IN THE PA

Toys

Popcorn

Dereen Taylor

Reading Borough Council

Explore the world with **Popcorn** - your complete first non-fiction library.

Look out for more titles in the **Popcorn** range. All books have the same format of simple text and striking images. Text is carefully matched to the pictures to help readers to identify and understand key vocabulary.
www.waylandbooks.co.uk/popcorn

First published in 2009 by Wayland
Reprinted in 2009 by Wayland

This paperback edition published in 2010
by Wayland
Reprinted in 2010 ,2011 and 2012 by Wayland

Copyright © Wayland 2009

Wayland
338 Euston Road
London NW1 3BH

Wayland Australia
Level 17/207 Kent Street
Sydney NSW 2000

Editor: Julia Adams
Designer: Alix Wood

British Library Cataloguing in Publication Data:
Taylor, Dereen
    Toys. - (Popcorn. In the past)
    1. Toys - History - Juvenile literature 2. Play - History -
    Juvenile literature
    I. Title
    688.7'2'09
    ISBN 978 0 7502 6423 5

Printed and bound in China

Wayland is a division of Hachette Children's Books,
an Hachette UK Company. www.hachette.co.uk

Acknowledgements:
J. Abecasis Collection/Topfoto: 1, 7.
Classic Stock/Topfoto: 4. English
Heritage/HIP/Topfoto: 6. J R
Eyerman/Time Life/ Getty Images: 13.
Cecil Higgins Gallery: 14. Hulton
Archive/Getty Images: 5. Hulton
Deutsch Collection/Corbis: 19.
Picturepoint/Topfoto: 10, 16, 17, 18, 20.
Topfoto: 11, 15, 21. Topical Press/Hulton
Archive/Getty Images: 2, 12. Eileen
Tweedy/Art Archive: front cover, 8. Toshi
Wakabayashi/amanaimages/Corbis: 9.
Andy Crawford: 23.

Contents

Dolls   4

Miniatures   6

War games   8

Transport   10

Boys and girls   12

Games and puzzles   14

Building toys   16

Outdoor games   18

Toys on wheels   20

Timeline   22

Make a toy car   23

Glossary   24

Index   24

Dolls

In the past, boys and girls
played with different toys.
Dolls were only for girls.

The clothes of these
beautiful Victorian dolls
were sewn by hand.

Girls from rich families had dolls with cloth bodies. The face and hands of the dolls made of wax or porcelain. Poor girls had dolls made from rags.

This girl's doll is made out of old clothes and sheets.

1935

Miniatures

Girls from rich families had lovely dolls' houses to play with. Each room had furniture to go in it.

How many bedrooms does this dolls' house have?

1830

6

Many girls had tiny tea sets to play tea parties with. They were made of china, just like real tea sets.

These girls are having a tea party with their dolls.

1910

War games

Boys played with toy soldiers. They were made of lead, wood or tin and were painted by hand.

These toy soldiers from 1820 are made of tin.

After World War II (1939-1945),
boys liked to play with military toys,
such as model fighter planes.

These model planes
look like the fighter
planes from the
World War II.

Transport

Many boys liked playing with model cars. These cars were made out of metal and they were big enough to ride in.

It was fun to drive a car that looked so real!

1947

Clockwork toys were invented in the 1800s. They moved when you wound them up with a special key.

This clockwork train moved around on a track.

1949

Boys and girls

Some toys, such as hoops and spinning tops, were popular with boys and girls.

1922

How do children play with hoops today?

Spinning tops were cheap to buy and easy to carry. They could be spun just about anywhere, even on the palm of your hand if you practised a lot!

Most spinning tops were made of wood.

1955

Games and puzzles

Rich children had a lot of room to play.
That is why they often had picture blocks
and jigsaw puzzles.

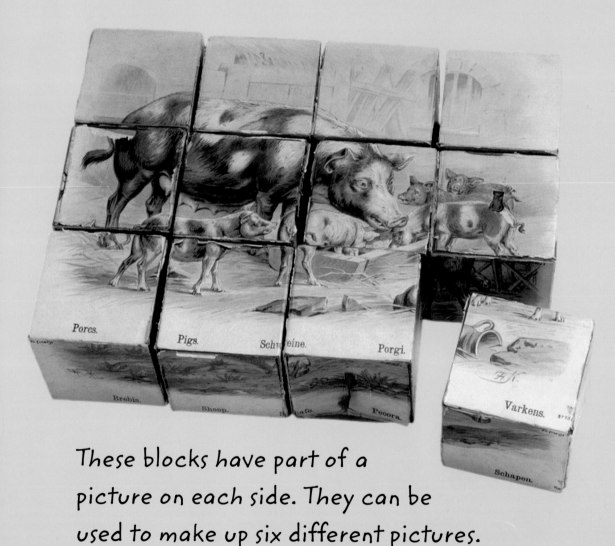

These blocks have part of a
picture on each side. They can be
used to make up six different pictures.

Many families enjoyed playing
board games together.

**Do you think
board games or
computer games
are more popular
today? Why?**

Monopoly was first played
in the 1930s and is still
around today.

Building toys

Meccano sets were invented in 1907 and became very popular. They were sets of nuts, bolts and metal strips with holes. You could build many different things with them.

This crane is made from a Meccano set.

Lego was invented in 1949 in Denmark.
It was one of the first toys made
of plastic.

1962

Lego pieces come in many different shapes and sizes. You can use them to build whole cities!

Outdoor games

Poor children had few toys to play with.
They lived in small, crowded homes,
so they often played outside.

There were less cars on the road. It was
safe for children to play in the streets.

1940

Many children liked skipping or playing with marbles. Another game children played was called five stones.

These children are playing a game of marbles.

Ask your grandparents what toys they had. Do you still play with any of them?

1920s

Toys on wheels

Children have always enjoyed being on the move. This is why scooters have been popular for more than 100 years!

How do these scooters look different to scooters today?

1930s

Many boys made go-karts out of old crates and pram wheels. It was almost as much fun making the go-kart as driving it!

1966

How is the driver steering this go-kart?

Timeline

1800s Clockwork toys are invented.

1870 The first ceramic marbles are produced.

1900s The first scooters are made.

1903 The first teddy bears go on sale.

1907 Meccano is invented.

1935 The first Monopoly board game is sold.

1940s Model cars made of metal are produced.

1945 After World War II, army toys become very popular.

1945 The first plastic toys are produced.

1949 Lego is invented in Denmark.

1959 A US company produces the first go-karts with motors.

1960s Companies start producing movable action figures.

Make a toy car

Make a toy car out of cardboard that can even drive.

You will need:

- a cardboard box (15cm x 15cm x3cm)
- a small piece of cardboard
- a black pen • a pencil
- paint and paint brushes
- paper fasteners
- scissors

1. Draw four circles on cardboard. Colour them in black.

2. Cut out the circles. Make a hole in the middle of each circle using your scissors.

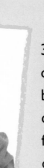

3. Mark a corner on the cardboard box. Cut out the corner. This is the front window of the car.

4. Make two holes along the bottom of both sides of the car using your scissors. Now you can paint your car.

5. Wait until the paint has dried. Use the paper fasteners to fix the wheels to your car.

6. Now your car is ready to play with!

23

Glossary

five stones   A game using five small stones. Four of the five stones are placed on the ground. The player throws the fifth stone into the air, and tries to pick up two of the stones on the ground before catching the fifth stone with the same hand.

military   To do with soldiers or the army.

plastic   A hard, lightweight material that comes in many different colours and shapes. A lot of today's toys are made of plastic.

porcelain   Special clay used to make thin, white pottery. The pottery is hard, but it can break easily. Some plates and tea cups are made of porcelain.

Victorian   Belonging to the time when Queen Victoria was on the throne (1837–1901).

wax   A natural material that is soft and melts easily. Candles are made of wax.

Index

board game 15
boys 4, 8, 9, 10, 12, 16

clockwork 11

doll 4, 5, 6, 7
dolls' house 6

game 14, 15, 18, 19
girls 4, 5, 6, 7, 12
go-kart 21

hoop 12

Lego 17

Meccano 16
military toy 8, 9
model car 10
Monopoly 15

poor 5, 18
puzzle 14

rich 5, 6

scooter 20
spinning top 13

toy 4, 5, 6, 7, 8, 9, 10, 11, 12, 13, 16, 17, 19, 20, 21

Victorian 4, 11

World War II 9